You See My
GLORY
but Not My
STORY

Carla Johnson

ISBN 978-1-64349-795-2 (paperback)
ISBN 978-1-64349-796-9 (digital)

Christian Faith Publishing, Inc.
832 Park Avenue
Meadville, PA 16335
www.christianfaithpublishing.com

Printed in the United States of America

I cry and pray at night so my family can smile in the morning. It's 3:00 a.m. My family is sleeping peacefully. I slowly remove the comforter from my body and ease out of bed, trying not to wake my husband. I walk into my bathroom closet and fall to my hands and knees in prayer. "But thou, when thou prayest, enter into thy closet, and when thou hast shut thy door, pray to thy Father which is in secret; and thy Father which seeth in secret shall reward thee openly" (Matt. 6:6 KJV). I thank God for another day. Praying in solitude has allowed me to become closer to God. As a young child, I witnessed my grandmother praying in her closet. I didn't understand why until I became older and began living my life as a Christian.

I can recall on several occasions walking into my bathroom or closet, kneeling in prayer. Oftentimes, I would not ask God for anything, but I would spend several minutes praising Him. I praised God for things that I used to take for granted. I would thank Him for my eyes to see, my arms to hug, my hands to hold, my legs to stand, and my feet to guide me. I would thank Him for being able to taste, see, hear, and feel. I often prayed for others to be healed. Many times tears would flow from my eyes because God's grace is so amazing, and I do not deserve His grace, yet He loves me in spite of my imperfections. I ask that you go to God in solitude—no noise or distractions, and just you and our Father. Don't ask for anything but thank Him for everything. I can't guarantee that your experience will be as surreal as mine. However, God wants us to come to Him in prayer. "The eyes of the LORD are on the righteous and His ears are attentive to their cry" (Ps. 34:15).

If you seek a relationship with God and try to follow and honor Him in your life, you, I, or no one will ever have to ask, is God listening to prayers? Psalm 34:14 assures us that he is carefully attuned to our lives and eager to hear every prayer that comes from our lips. One thing I can promise: you have nothing to lose.

Several stages in my life trials and tribulations seemed to consume me. If my husband wasn't in turmoil, it was my children. If it wasn't either of them, my parents' health was failing. My mom fell, broke her nose, and suffered a concussion. My dad was diagnosed with kidney cancer, and my health began to fail. My sister and her family were in a car accident, she also suffered a heart attack, and my brother suffered a severe stroke, which left him paralyzed on his left side. My son was laid off from his job shortly after my grandson was born. My daughter was homeschooled because of bullying, which caused her to be severely depressed.

Please don't misunderstand me. I'm not complaining, just explaining. I can assure you that you are not alone no matter what you are going through.

Nevertheless, my entire life felt as though it was falling apart piece by piece. I witnessed God's grace through it all. I always thank God for allowing me the opportunity to praise him on my knees. I praise God through the good and bad. Is it easy? Absolutely not. Many people see your glory and not your story. I pray that you will be blessed. This is my story.

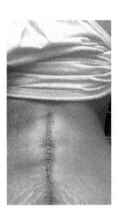

It was only six months ago when I was confined to a wheelchair. I lost total use of my legs because of a large synovial cyst, which was growing on my lumbar spine between discs L4 and L5. I was also diagnosed with spondylolisthesis, a condition in which the bone in my vertebrae slid forward and compressed the nerve roots and spinal cord; and a severe degenerative disc disease also attacked my spine, causing a change in the structure of my spine. My trials and tribulations at an early age allowed me to thirst for God's word and his will.

Only God Can Judge

My life was simple and exciting until November 10, 1980, my fifteenth birthday. I was lying on my bed talking to Roland Roberts, our new basketball captain and track star. He transferred from Madison High School. He was tall, dark, and extremely handsome. Roland and I talked almost every night for two months. We ate lunch together Monday through Friday in the school cafeteria. One day, while eating lunch, Roland asked me to go to Astroworld, one of the best amusement parks in Houston, Texas. I thought to myself, *Oh my God! The Boogie Boys are performing next month at Astroworld. Everyone will be there. Maybe my mom would consider chaperoning.* The thought of my mom showing up at the amusement park caused me to experience an instant pain on the left side of my chest. I grabbed my left breast because the pain was very intense. I didn't want to end my conversation with Roland, so I continued to gently rub my chest and left breast. While doing so, I felt a golf-ball-sized lump in my breast.

Two weeks before my sweet sixteen, I wasn't concerned about my breast. I had more important things on my agenda. What am I going to wear Saturday? What are the majorettes going to say when I tell them that Roland Roberts, the handsome basketball captain, asked me on a date? Will my parents approve? Most of all, will they want to chaperone? The week before my date with Roland, I made sure I completed my chores and homework and helped my mom around the house. When I asked for my parents' permission, they agreed. I told Roland that my mom was dropping me off at the front gates of the amusement park between 4:00 p.m. and 4:30 p.m.

As a fifteen-year-old, you want everything to be perfect. I changed clothes six times. I decided to wear a pink tank top, blue jean shorts, white Ken Rosewall tennis shoes, and white footies with the pink ball on the back. When I arrived, I noticed him right away. I was mesmerized by his appearance. I've never seen him outside of school before. He was talking to a group of guys. He was wearing a blue-and-white T-shirt, khaki shorts, and white Converse tennis shoes. As I was walking toward him, he turned toward me and smiled. He has chocolate brown skin, beautiful white teeth, and a dimple in his left check. He stood about six feet tall with broad muscular shoulders, black wavy hair, and long eyelashes. As he walked toward me, I noticed he was bowlegged. Most people would consider that a flaw, but it was very attractive to me. When he neared me, he held his arms out to give me a hug. I was so nervous I tripped and fell to the ground on my hands and knees. A group of girls standing at the ticket counter were laughing and pointing at me. I scraped a small amount of skin from my knees and the palm of my left hand. I was bleeding slightly. Roland tried to catch me, but he wasn't close enough. As I lay on the ground, I looked up at him. I witnessed him trying to hold back tears of laughter. He said, "Oh my God are you okay?"

I said, "No!" I noticed immediately he became concerned.

He said, "I'm so sorry. I didn't realize you were hurt."

I whispered to him, "I'm not hurt physically, but I'm extremely embarrassed. I don't want to get up. I'm going to pretend that I fainted."

He said, "No worries, everyone out here has fallen before."

He helped me up, and we walked over to the water fountain and washed the dirt off my hands and knees. Once I regained my composure, Roland looked down at me and said jokingly, "Astroworld should repair those invisible steps before someone really injures themselves. I tripped two or three times on those exact steps. So there's no need to be embarrassed or want to pretend to faint. No one out here can judge you. Only God is capable of doing that. First Corinthians 4:3–4 states: 'But with me it is a very small thing that I should be judged by you or by any human court. In fact, I do not even judge myself. For I am not aware of anything against myself, but I am not thereby acquitted. It is the Lord who judges me.'" After Roland said that, it seemed as though I liked him even more. I had seldom heard a teenager mention God's name in such a relaxed and profound way.

I told him that I needed to purchase my ticket. He held up two tickets and said, "I've taken care of it." We entered into the gates of the park. It appeared as though everyone from our school was there. We rode the Grease Lightning, the Texas Cyclone, and the Gun Slinger just to name a few; he bought us burgers and fries. It seemed as though I had known him my entire life.

Finally 8:00 p.m. arrived, and the doors to the Boggie Fog opened. The Boogie Boys were singing most of the hip-hop songs of the eighties. Dancing had always been my passion. We stood around and talked to friends for ten to fifteen minutes. He said, "Beautiful young lady, would you like to dance with me?"

I said, "Sure."

As we were walking to the dance floor, he told me to watch out for the invisible steps. We both laughed. I wasn't sure if he could dance. I decided to follow his lead. He stood in one place and said, "Let me see what you can do." I started off with a popular dance called the Snake and followed it with the Freak. He smiled and said, "You have skills." He started dancing. He moved to every single beat. I asked how he learned to dance so well. He told me that he loved dancing since he was a toddler.

We danced nonstop from eight thirty until nine forty-five. He raised his shirt up to wipe his face. Holy smokes, this boy has a six-pack. I told him to stop showing off because he didn't have to raise his shirt. He said, "I'm not showing off. I just wiped sweat out of my eyes." He raised his shirt, and he began to roll his stomach like a belly dancer. I almost fainted. I never saw a stomach move like that before. I covered my eyes like a two-year-old. It looked great. I said to myself this guy is a show off. He raised his shirt up and continued to roll his stomach while looking into my eyes. I wasn't sure if he was trying to be sexy or thought I could belly dance. I said, "I can barely hold my stomach in when my pants are too tight. Therefore, I'm not going to even try to roll my stomach. I think it's time for me to go home." I felt extremely awkward.

As we were walking out of the exit gates, they announced on the intercom that the Boogie Fog would be closing in fifteen minutes. He grabbed my hand and asked me to be his girlfriend. I couldn't believe what I was hearing. I looked at him and said, "Are you sure?"

He said, "I can't stop thinking about you when we are apart. I would like for us to date and get to know everything about each other."

I said, "Yes, I would really like to be your girlfriend."

We hugged, and he tried to kiss me. I pulled away and gave him a pat on the shoulder and said good-bye. I couldn't imagine what punishment I would endure if my parents would have witnessed me kissing a boy in public. A pat on the back and a friendly hug were all that I could contribute to our amazing first date.

Oh, God, No, Not My Breast

The following week, I was on the phone talking to Roland when my mom walked into my room and said she wanted to talk to me. I knew she was uncomfortable yet concerned. She leaned on the door panel as she played with the ends of her hair. I noticed she appeared to be worried. I told Roland that I would call him back. I asked my mom what was on her mind. She said she was concerned about me because my breasts were getting extremely large. She asked me if I was sexually active or if I had been playing with my breast. My mom is a sweetheart, but she has a way of getting straight to the point.

I immediately became defensive. I said I've had a boyfriend for less than a month. I am afraid to hold his hand in public in fear that you or dad might witness and embarrass me. I said, "Mom, we haven't kissed yet. Sex? I haven't consider having sex! I don't want a baby!" My mom talked to my sister and me about sex at least once a month. She kept track of our menstrual cycles better than we did. During that time of the month, she would pay close attention to our hygiene. She drilled us in cleanliness. She always said when a woman is menstruating, no one should know. "If someone walks into the bathroom after you've cleaned up, there should be no evidence that you are having your menstrual cycle." My sister and I had our on personal lady bags, which contained everything a young lady needed during that time of month.

Mom talked to us openly about birth control. I looked forward to my mom coming into our room for our monthly meetings. My sister and I shared our bedroom. We had twin beds that sat across from each other with a small night stand that separated the beds. We had a dresser that sat against the wall near the foot of our beds. Mom would come in our room; sit on the dresser; and talk to us about sex, life, school, and whatever topic she felt was important during that particular month.

We talked about every birth control method that was known in the eighties. Before leaving our room, she would turn to us and say, "The only sure way you will not get pregnant or infected with a sexually transmitted disease is to never have sex."

As for as me playing with my breast, I have never considered doing that! Honestly, I think it's really gross! I said the lump in my breast is probably the reason they look bigger. The look on Mom's face appeared as though she witnessed the ghost of Christmas Past. Her face was flushed, and her eyes were wide and fixed on me. It appeared as though she almost went into a trance. There was complete silence for a minute. She said, "Victoria, you have lumps in your breast?" It was a question of surprise and being startled at the same time. She asked me a series of questions, "Are there lumps anywhere else on your body? Did you injure yourself? Are you in pain?"

I answered, "No, no, no, and no."

She said, "This is not a joke! Why didn't you tell me? You have to be more detailed than a one-word response."

I said, "Mom, it's okay. I meant to tell you, but I've been busy with dance, majorette practice, and school [as you would think any teenager might be]. I totally forgot." I told her the lumps weren't painful, so I didn't think much about them.

My mom told my dad. He came into my room, hugged me, and said, "Hey, Peaches, let's go for a ride."

Going for a ride with my dad was one the most awesome and memorable moments of my young-adult years. My dad drove extremely slow. Oftentimes I'm sure he would coast to most of our destinations. The ride from our house to Dairy Queen would take most drivers ten minutes, but my dad and I would take twice as long. He said he drove under the speed limit because he would never forgive himself if he hurt a child playing in the street or an animal crossing the street. I said, "Dad, we are on Cullen Boulevard, one of the busiest streets in Southeast Houston." I don't think a child would be playing in the street.

He would look at me and say, "Well, I'm in no hurry. That's what's wrong with young people. You guys are always in a hurry. Just slow down and enjoy life and what God has blessed you with, which is waking up to a beautiful new day, because somewhere someone did not get this opportunity."

My dad has a unique way with words, yet he has the most adorable way of getting his point across. I must admit that most of his hard work and ethics have stuck with me. I enjoyed our long car rides. We would talk about sports, his job, school, anything that interest us. I frequently enjoyed the talks about the Houston Oilers and how Earl Campbell would run through players like he was a human bulldozer. I also liked the stories of how he would switch trains from different tracks. My dad was dedicated to his job and family. He retired from Southern Pacific with 35 years of service.

We pulled into Dairy Queen and ordered our favorite comfort food: a large fry and a cup of ice cream. I would dip a fry into my vanilla ice cream and allow it to dance with my taste buds. I'm aware that this is a strange combination, but it has always satisfied me. He told me that he was going to use all the strength, resources, hopes, and dreams that God has given him in order for me to live a healthy, pain-free life.

We sat and ate in silence for a few minutes. This stocky, muscular man, my dad, looked at me with tears in his eyes and said, "You are going to be okay."

I was so confused. I smiled, nodded, and said in a low whisper, "Yes, I know I'm going to be okay, Dad. What God has in store for me is for me." I know whatever he has in store, he will see me through.

Yet deep within my heart of hearts, I was confused. My mom was crying. My dad promised me that everything would be okay and not to worry. What they didn't understand was I felt great! I had a boyfriend, I was a majorette captain and an honor student, and my friends were envious. Yes, life was great.

Later that night, I could not sleep. My parents' actions made me very concerned. That night, I walked into my closet, closed the door, and kneeled in prayer. I recalled John 10:10 (KJV). Jesus said, "I came that you may have life and have it abundantly—a complete life of purpose." I felt that my life had great purpose. Why? Because God made me in his divine image.

The following week, I was in the band room listening to cadences with a few of the drummers and my best friend, Sarah, who was head flagette for the Worthing Colts Marching Band. Suddenly via the school intercom, I was summoned to the front office and was instructed to bring my belongings because I was leaving for the entire afternoon. I did not understand why my mom picked me up early from school. Maybe she decided to schedule my doctor's appointment on a Tuesday. I don't think she understood that I had to choreograph a dance for our next football game, which was less than a week away. As a teenager, I thought she was being insensitive.

As she drove to the medical center, it was obvious she was concerned. She was quiet and focused. She did not turn the radio on or ask about my day. I was upset because I was having a great time with Sarah and the drummers and I had several ideas for our next majorette routine, yet I was on my way to the doctor to have my breast examined, and there's nothing wrong with me. Oh boy, was I wrong.

We finally arrived at the Diagnostic Center of Houston. It was a tall brown brick building that sat in the middle of the Texas Medical Center on Fannin Avenue. It was located on the southeast side of Hermann Hospital. My mom drove into the parking garage. The attendant said, "Ten dollars please." I thought my mom was going to complain about the price of the medical center's parking. She did not say anything, gave the money to the attendant, and drove away.

I said to myself, *Wow, this is serious. Mom always complains when she has to pay for parking.*

We parked and rode the elevator to the twelfth floor. Once we arrived, I noticed the office was about nine hundred square feet and surrounded by smoked glass. It was decorated in mint green, gray, and silver. As my mom checked me in, I walked to the window and was able to see most of downtown Houston. I was sitting in the waiting room and noticed there were men and women of all ages.

About twenty minutes passed, and finally, a petite lady opened the door and called my name. She had long brown hair and hazel eyes. We made eye contact, and her smile and demeanor gave me a sense of calmness. She told me to get undressed from the waist up. I removed my shirt and bra and sat on the end of the examining table, anticipating on what was about to transpire. Shortly afterward, Dr. Smith entered the room. He was tall with big green eyes and gray hair. He was dressed as immaculate as his office. Dr. Smith was very nice and personable. He introduced himself and asked me what my plans were after high school. He explained to me the type of exam he was going to perform and why. He asked me if I have any questions or concerns and told me if for some reason I felt uncomfortable let him know. He asked me to lie on the examining table while he performed the exam. He examined my breasts with the pads of his finger. He moved his fingers in a circular motion on each breast. He asked me if I was sore or in pain. I assured him that I wasn't. He informed me that he was trying to locate any lumps or nodules. His nurse was also in the exam room. Suddenly he told her in a stern tone, "Order an ultrasound stat." He looked at me with a smile, yet I could tell he was very concerned. He asked me to get dressed. The nurse called radiology while he gave us directions on how to get there. My mom and I walked down to radiology, which was on the tenth floor. The nurse told my mom that the doctor would call us in three to five days with my results.

I returned to school Wednesday, and everyone was asking me if I was okay because my mom picked me up early the day before. I assured them that I never felt better.

While having lunch, the student office assistance walked up to me and said, "Your parents are here, and you have to leave for the day." I thought it was all a joke. I walked to the office and saw Principal Baines and my parents. They appeared to be very concerned. They looked as though I was sentenced to death row. I said, "Oh my God, what's wrong?"

My mom walked up to me and said, "The nurse from the doctor's office called, and they want you to have the lump removed from your breast. Your surgery is scheduled for Thursday morning."

I said, "I have to have surgery tomorrow? No, this can't be happening! I feel great! I'm not in pain!"

My mom was so calm and said, "Exactly, and that's why they want the foreign object removed from your body in order to prevent pain."

I said, "Dad, do I have to leave now?"

He said, "Yes, Sweet Peaches, we have no other alternative."

I asked them if they could allow me a minute to say good-bye to my friends. Principal Baines agreed, and I walked down the hallway as I fought back tears. I finally made it to the girls' bathroom. I checked the stalls to see if anyone was inside. I prayed Psalm 119:28, "My soul is weary with sorrow. Strengthen me according to your word. God, I don't know what is happening to me, but I know you will never leave me or forsake me." I wiped the tears from my eyes, combed my hair, adjusted my clothes, and proceeded to walk down the hall into the band room.

I said good-bye to my friends. They could not believe that I had to have surgery. They continued to say, "You don't look sick. You look great. Are you sure you are having surgery?" I assured them that surgery was necessary. Everyone said they would take lots of pictures at the game and visit me while I recovered.

On the way home, we stopped for ice cream and french fries. I will admit it made me feel better, yet I could not help but wonder, why me? We finally arrived home, and my brother and sister were still in school. I walked into my room and packed my bags before letting my parents know that I was prepared to leave. I went into the hall bathroom across from our room that I shared with my sister. I kneeled on the side of the bathtub and began to pray Jeremiah 17:14 (NIV), "Heal me, Lord, and I will be healed." "The LORD will guard you're going out and you're coming in from this time forth and forever" (Ps. 121:8 KJV).

My parents and I arrived at Hermann Hospital and were instructed to go to the admissions desk. The hospital representative placed a band on my arm and directed us to the seventh floor. The representative informed me that I would be in room 723B, and a nurse would meet us there to inform me about my surgical procedure. I walked into my new temporary residence and noticed it was occupied by an older lady who was lying on her back. She had several monitors around her. She had an oxygen tube in her nose, and machines were beeping as small red and green lights were flashing. I turned around and told my parents that I could not go inside. It felt as though my feet were cemented to the floor as I stood in the hallway. I felt that my new roommate would not survive until morning. I said, "Dad, please don't make me sleep in there."

He looked at me and said, "There's no way I would make you endure this."

My parents and I walked downstairs to the admissions office and requested a private room. The representative informed my parents that the insurance deductible for a private room would cost $250. I recalled on the way to the hospital my dad told my mom that he withdrew $300 from their account in order to pay the car note and buy groceries for my brother and sister. I knew he had other obligations, yet he did not hesitate to pay the deductible in order for me to be comfortable.

Once again, we returned to the seventh floor and entered a new room several doors away. This room was furnished with a single bed, soft blue-and-white curtains, sofa recliner, and 24-inch colored television. I thanked my parents and assured them that I was extremely grateful.

That night I couldn't sleep. I began to pray over and over. "In peace I will lie down and sleep, for you alone, Lord, make me dwell in safety" (Ps. 4:8 NIV).

I went into surgery the following day. When I awoke from recovery, my family and friends were there. My chest was wrapped extremely tight. I reached to feel for my breasts, but they weren't there! I started screaming and crying uncontrollably. "What happened to my breasts? They took my breasts!"

My mom gently grabbed my face and said, "Victoria, look into my eyes. Look at me, sweetheart."

I looked at her, and she told me that no one had taken my breast. They both were there but were bandaged and wrapped because of the surgery.

Everything happened so fast. I felt as though my head was spinning. How could this be? I felt like the man in Mark 9:24 (NKJV): "Lord, I believe, but help my unbelief." One day I was one of the most popular freshmen at my school, and the next week I was lying in the hospital with bandages around my breasts. I could barely move.

Later that night, after everyone left, I asked my mom if there was a Bible in the hospital room. She reached in the drawer, opened the Bible, and handed it to me. It was the King James Version of the Holy Bible. It was opened to Isaiah 53:3: "But he was wounded for our transgressions, he was bruised for our iniquities; the chastisement of our peace was upon him, and with his stripes we are healed." You see, no matter what stumbling blocks I encounter, the Holy Bible has always been there to clear my understanding and let me know that the roads may seem rough or rugged but God has a plan for me.

I was in the hospital for several days. I completed four weeks of radiation therapy, which made me extremely weak. The radiation therapy was administered to stop the growth of any remaining cancer cells. It can be used alone or in combination with surgery, chemotherapy, or both. It left me feeling nauseous and weak. My mom explained to me that this was part of my healing process, which would prevent the foreign object from returning. Roland was at the hospital with me every day. He would bring my class assignments and homework. He never mentioned anything about my hair or weight loss. Every day he would tell me how beautiful and brave I was.

Once I was released from the hospital, I was on bed rest for two weeks. I called my cousin Todd, who was a hairdresser, and he agreed to cut my hair into a short style. When I returned to school, everyone admired my new cut. I unknowingly increased Todd's clientele.

I felt sick every day for the first six weeks after returning to school. I did not share my physical or emotional feelings with anyone. I didn't want pity or sympathy. I just wanted to be treated like everyone else. Thank God, things finally began to fall back into place. I was enjoying school, my grades were good, and Roland and I had become best friends.

Why, God, Why?

My senior year 1984, I was voted and won Most Beautiful and Best Dressed. I was nominated for Prom Queen and won Homecoming Queen. I was head majorette. I had the boyfriend who I thought all the girls wanted. I was starting Prairie View A&M University the summer of 1984 in hopes of pursuing my nursing degree. Roland told me that he did not want to attend college. He dreamed of becoming a firefighter, and college was not in his plans. I told Roland that I respected his decision, but I've always dreamed of going to college. I enrolled into Prairie View A&M nursing program. My first semester I completed seventeen hours with a 3.7 GPA. Nothing could stop me now—at least that's what I thought.

I was in Banks Hall, taking a shower, and decided to perform my monthly breast exam. Thanks to Dr. Smith, I knew how to complete a self-exam and did so every month. I used my left hand, moved the pads of my fingers around my right breast, and gently in small circular motions covered the entire breast area and armpit. I used light, medium, and firm pressure. I squeezed my nipple and checked for discharge and lumps. I repeated this same procedure on my right breast. My exam was almost complete. Oh my God! I felt another lump, much bigger than the first one. *What is happening to me? What have I done to deserve this?* "'For I know the plans I have for you,' declares the LORD, 'plans to prosper you and not to harm you plans to give you hope and a future'" (Jer. 29:11 KJV). I could not understand why this was happening to me. I called my mom and told her that I felt another lump in my right breast. She was very calm and caring. She told me to pray and believe that God has a plan for me no matter what the circumstances are.

The following Friday I had another appointment with Dr. Smith. As he was examining me, I noticed an expression of concern on his face. He looked down at me then over at my mother. I knew whatever it was it wasn't good. He removed his gloves and asked my mom and me to see him in his office. As I was getting dressed, I told my mother that I was terrified and I did not want to hear the results of my exam. My mom told me to stay in the waiting room and she would talk to the doctor alone. As I sat there, I began to pray. I began praying James 1:2–4 (KJV): "Consider it pure joy, my brother and sisters, whenever you face trials of any kinds, because you know that the testing of your faith produces perseverance, Let perseverance finish its work so that you may be mature and complete, not lacking anything."

It seemed like a lifetime, but my mom returned to the waiting room after about thirty minutes. I asked her if I had to have surgery. She told me that I had to have the foreign object removed from my breast. I fell to my knees and said, "Oh God, no no no!" I was screaming! "I can't go through this again! What am I going to do about school? Will I have to withdraw from college? Can I just leave whatever it is inside of me? I promise I will let them take it out if it gets bigger. Mom, please don't make me do this again! I can't! I just can't put my life on hold again!"

My mom kneeled down on the floor with me and said ever so softly, "Baby girl, look at Mamma." She was so calm as she gently wiped the tears from my eyes. I began to calm down. I looked at her. She quoted 1 Thessalonians 5:18, "Give thanks in all circumstances, for this is God's will for you in Christ Jesus."

I said, "You are right. I believe and trust in God, but it seems as though all my friends are enjoying their life and I can't seem to stay healthy. Is God mad at me?"

My mom said, "No, He's not mad or displeased with you. Victoria, what does the word *but* do?"

I wiped my face again and said with a tremble in my voice, "It cancels out everything you said before. Why do you ask?"

My mom said, "Victoria, you told me that you believe and trust in God, *but* your friends are enjoying their lives and you can't seem to stay healthy. So have you canceled out the fact that you believe in God and the plan He has for you?"

I said, "No, that's not what I meant, yet as a child of God, I want to know why this is happening to me."

She said, "Why not you?"

I said, "Because I haven't done anything to deserve this." I was beginning to lose my faith. Yet again, I felt like the man in Mark 9:24: "Lord, I believe, but help my unbelief."

My mom said, "Let's go for a walk."

We were in the Houston Diagnostic Professional Building. We walked a few blocks in silence until we came to Ben Taub Hospital emergency room. I said, "Why are we here?" My mom did not say anything as the doors to the ER slid open. There were people young and old waiting to be treated. I recalled a young lady sitting in a wheelchair with torn clothes and bruises throughout her body. She was holding a towel to her head and bleeding. I heard her tell the nurse that she was pushed out of the car by her boyfriend, and she had no money or family. A couple ran in screaming because their three-month-old infant's fever was 103 degrees and he went into convulsions. They said they did not bring him in earlier because they had no money, transportation, or health insurance; but over-the-counter medications only made his condition worse. A family was huddled together comforting one another because the doctor informed them that their loved one did not survive surgery. I said, "Mom, can we please leave now?"

She said, "Do you understand?"

I said, "Yes, more than ever." I recalled Romans 5:3–5: "More than that we rejoice in our suffering produce endurance and endurance produces character and charter produces hope and hope does not put us to shame because God's love has been poured into our hearts through the Holy Spirit who has been given to us." As we walked backed to the parking garage, I thought to myself, *I'm sure those people asked God the same question. "Why me?"*

Holy Oil and Prayer

Our grandmother

*W*hen my mom and I returned home, my dad, sister, and brother were there. My mom explained to them that I had to have another surgery and my recovery time in the hospital was three to five days. They started to hug me and reassure me that I would be okay. My mom said, "Yes, she will be just fine. Now get yourselves together. We need to visit Big Mamma [the name that we used for our grandmother] before it's too late."

My grandparents went to bed before seven every night. Once we arrived to my grandmother's house, I headed straight for the phone. I wanted to call Roland and tell him that I was home for the weekend. As I was talking to Roland, my Big Mama walked into the bedroom. She was a beautiful, dark-brown-skinned woman. She was petite, approximately five feet four inches, with short black hair. No matter what time we visited her, she cooked for us and always greeted us with a warm, loving hug. There was never a doubt in my mind that my grandparents LOVED me! She put her arms around me, and as she was hugging me, she poured a small amount of oil onto the crown of my head. I will never forget the distinct smell. It was a mixture of lavender and frankincense, a fruity aroma. I said, "Big Mamma, what was that?"

She said, "Just a little holy oil, baby. Big Mamma just wanted to anoint you today, but never forget I pray a special prayer for you daily."

Growing up, attending church with my Big Mamma, and listening to her pray and speak in tongue were absolutely amazing to me. There were two other prayer warriors I have been blessed to love and receive love from in return: Una Johnson and Madeline Harper. I believe that they were angels that God sent to watch over us and keep the family grounded. Everything that they endured, I never saw or heard either of them complain or question their circumstances. "For where two or three are gathered together in my name, I am there in the midst of them" (Matt. 18:20 KJV). One day I will be as strong in my faith as my three prayer warriors.

Roland said he also had a praying grandmother. Laughing to myself, I said, "Maybe so. However, my three prayer warriors can pray the devil out of hell."

He said, "No, I don't think my Nana is that prayerful."

I told him that was sheer exaggeration, but they never worried or complained. Their faith in God is admired and respected by many people throughout the church and community.

I talked to Roland the entire time we were visiting my grandparents. We decided to go to the movies on Saturday in order to clear my head. Sunday I returned back to school. I asked my mom when I needed to register for surgery. She said, "Maybe a week from today."

This would give me time to talk to my professors and try to complete my courses early so I would not have to withdraw from my classes and lose credits.

Monday morning, as I was getting ready for class, my phone rang. It was my mom. She said, "Victoria, Dr.'s Smith office called, and you need to register for the hospital today. Your surgery is scheduled for Wednesday."

I said, "What! Are you serious?" I immediately became angry. I thought of James 1:20 (NIV), "Human anger does not produce the righteousness that God desires," yet I could not hold back my anger or frustration. I said, "Mom, you told me that I had several days! Now you're telling me that I need to miss class, come home, and register for the hospital?"

She said, "Yes, sweetheart, that's exactly what I am saying."

I slammed the phone down without saying good-bye. I was crying almost uncontrollably, and my face was covered in tears. I allowed frustration to consume me. I began pulling clothes off the hangers from my closet and throwing them into my trunk. I was yelling, "I'm tired, God! I believe! I worship you! What am I doing wrong? Please, God, please tell me! I can't do this anymore. Send me a sign! Why is this happening to me over and over? God, I don't have the strength."

Shortly afterward, there was a knock on my door. I said, *Oh God, who and what is it now?*

I unlocked the door and swung it open with a face filled with tears. I couldn't believe my eyes! It was my mom, dad, sister, brother, and Roland. My dad said, "You have to come home, Sweet Peaches, but not alone." That was the best feeling ever. I sobbed out of relief that I was not alone. My mom, brother, Roland, and I packed my things while my sister and dad withdrew me from the university. That was one of the hardest things I've ever had to do, but I knew it was for the best.

Wednesday I went into surgery. Before surgery, Roland told me that it was too much for him to bear, and he felt we should be friends. He said he felt guilty going to parties and hanging out with friends and I wasn't there with him. I was totally shocked by this news. I told him that I cared deeply for him, and my declining health wasn't my fault, just my fate. He said he could only see me as his friend. I said to myself, *Victoria, no matter what you say or do, you cannot keep a man who does not want to be kept.*

I had too much to deal with. Roland was tertiary on my list of concerns. I cared deeply for him, but I understood that he had to do what he felt was right for him. After all, self-preservation is the first law of nature; people think of themselves first. They fight for survival and/or seek peace. Roland was in search for peace and self-satisfaction. I understood and appreciated his honesty. I was going through a lot. I felt he did the right thing.

That next day I went into surgery. The process wasn't as terrifying as the first time because I knew what to expect. Was it easy? Of course not. My body was weaker. My breast was even smaller because they removed a cyst the size of a plum, and again, they removed the tissue around my breast in order for them to perform a biopsy. The recovery time was four to six weeks. This gave Satan just enough time to convince me that I should not go back to school. After, I healed from the second breast surgery. I decided that I was not going to return to Prairie View A&M. I began working at a clothing store. I knew this wasn't my dream, want, or desire for my life. But I was at a standstill.

God, Please Don't Take My Sight

Almost three months into feeling healthy and hospital free, I awoke and noticed that my left eye was draining and very irritated. I asked my sister if she was seen something in my eye. She said, "Oh my God, what is that?" I ran to the mirror, pulled my eyelid up, and noticed a bump the size of a pea on the inside of my eyelid.

I ran into the room and woke my parents. My mom looked at my eye and said, "Get dressed, baby girl. You need to see the doctor."

We went to the emergency room. By this time, I had a terrible headache. My eye was swollen, red, and extremely painful. The hospital clerk called me and my mom to the desk and asked what was going on. I removed the ice pack and lifted my eyelid. The nurse almost fell back into her chair. She looked at my mom and said, "I'm going to be completely honest. I'm not sure what's going on, but we will find out."

Three different doctors came into the room to assess me. Finally, doctor number four informed us that a large cyst had formed in my eye and I was going to need surgery immediately. I did not cry. I did not ask God why. I said, "Okay, I'm ready."

The nurse said, "I must admit I've never seen anyone this eager for surgery."

I said, "Ma'am, I am not eager at all. I have begun to understand Galatians 2:20. I have been crucified with Christ, and it is no longer I who live, but Christ lives in me and the life I now live in the flesh. I live by faith in the Son of God who loved me and gave himself up for me."

She looked at my mom and said, "You have an amazing daughter."

My mom said, "You have no idea how amazing she really is."

My mom contacted the family and informed them that I was going to be admitted into the hospital. The surgery was the following morning. I was in the hospital for three days. I had to wear a patch on my eye for twenty-one days. Thank God, the cyst was removed successfully. When family and friends came to visit, they would ask me, "Are you in pain?" I always assured them that I was okay. I tried to stay in good spirits and look my best at all times. Not sure how good I looked with a patch on my eye, but if I had to tell you, I think I looked cute. Yet no one knew that I suffered from migraines the entire twenty-one days of healing. I tried to camouflage my pain. My sister was amazing during my healing process. She wouldn't turn the light on if I was resting. She would check books out from the school library and read them to me at night. She always assured me that a tough time doesn't last but tough people do.

From the Train to Abdominal Pain

*M*y older sister told me that my mom was planning a trip for the entire family. I was excited. I needed a change of pace. After several weeks of recovery, I was ready to leave Houston. We rode the train from Houston to Cincinnati, Ohio, to visit family. We had a great time. It seemed as though things were getting back to normal. My eyesight was great. No abnormalities were found during my breast self-exams. I was thinking about enrolling back into school. As we were preparing to leave the hotel, I experienced a sharp pain in my lower abdomen. My brother grabbed me before I fell to the ground. Our dad ran outside and packed me back into the hotel room. I laid down until my family finished packing. My mom gave me hot tea and pain meds. On the way to Houston, I was able to rest in the sleeping quarters on the train. It was small but more comfortable than sitting in the passenger train car.

Once we returned home, Mom told me that she was going to make an appointment for me to see Dr. Smith. I assured her that I felt better and might have experienced severe menstrual cramps. She agreed. Approximately two days later, we were in Kmart Department Store purchasing T-shirts for my dad and brother. My mom asked me to look for a pack of extralarge T-shirts because she could not find my dad's size on the opposite side of the table where she was. As I was leaning over the table, searching through the packages of T-shirts, I experienced an excruciating pain in my lower abdomen. It felt as though a six-foot two-hundred-pound man kicked me in my stomach with steel-toe boots. I said, "Oh Jesus! Oh my God! Mom, please help me!" My Big Mamma said when you don't have time to pray, call on the name of Jesus. I just began to whisper His holy name, "Jesus, Jesus, Jesus, oh, Jesus, please, please, Jesus, it's my stomach."

I was leaning on the table. My mom dropped the T-shirts and ran around to the other side of the table where I was barely standing. She told me to put my arm around her neck. I tried several times but did not have the strength to do so. I shook my head no. I felt myself drifting away. I was trying to say, "I think I'm going to faint or die." I was not sure what was happening to me, but one thing's for sure: I was drifting away fast. I tried desperately to speak and explain what was happening, but nothing would come out. I could only stare at my mom. I heard her scream for help. The last thing I recalled were three workers in their store uniforms, red shirts and black pants, running toward me. Seconds later, I passed out. I woke up in the ambulance. A young female paramedic put something under my nose, and it almost choked me. I started coughing, and I could hear my mom's voice reciting the Twenty-Third Psalm, but I could not see her. I asked the lady if my mom was with me, and she said yes. I looked up, and my mom was sitting behind my head, facing the rear of the ambulance.

They transported me to Hermann Hospital. My blood pressure and heart rate were high because of the severity of my pain. While in the ER, they ran several tests. Thank God, Dr. Smith was on duty that afternoon. He walked into the room holding the X-ray of my stomach. He told us that I had several cysts on both ovaries. They were so plentiful that he might have to remove one of my ovaries. He also stated that he was very concerned about one cyst that was located on my left ovary. He said it appeared to be a complex cyst, which is a solid or fluid-filled sac or pocket (cyst) within or on the surface of my ovary. He explained that the cyst had to be removed, and biopsies were going to be performed because of the tumor he removed from my breast. He said that if the cyst was cancerous, he would have to remove the entire ovary. I said, "That means I will never experience childbirth!"

He said, "Victoria, I know this must be very difficult for you, but I am obligated to try to save your life. Just remember this is what the tests are revealing. I will know more once we are in the operating room."

I asked Dr. Smith, "Is there some type of body scan that can detect everything that's wrong with me, fix it, and allow me to live my life? I'm tired of spending every other month in the hospital, and I know my parents are tired."

My mom looked at me and said, "You speak for yourself, young lady. Lamentations 3:22–23 says—and I believe—the steadfast of the Lord never ceases. His mercies never come to an end. They are new every morning. Great is your faithfulness."

I understood what my mom was saying. I also thought about the walk we took through the corridors of Ben Taub Hospital.

Two days after arriving to Herman Hospital emergency room, I was scheduled for surgery. Again, by the grace of God, my surgery was a success. He removed several cysts from my ovaries, and the largest one was not cancerous. He told me and my mom that he wasn't sure if my womb and ovaries were healthy enough for me to experience childbirth. My mom held back tears. I told Dr. Smith that I had a great amount of respect for him, and with God working through him, he saved my life. However, I will not believe that God would not allow me to experience childbirth.

Several years later, I was blessed with my son and daughter. My pregnancy with my son was extremely complicated. Everything was going great. My baby was active. I was elated because I was experiencing a healthy pregnancy until my twenty-eighth-week checkup. After my examination, Dr. Palmer asked me to get dressed and come into her office. I thought she was going to prescribe me medication for my severe back pain. I know that sounds insane, but that's exactly what I was thinking. When I found out I was pregnant with my son, I was 110 pounds. I gained seventy-five pounds by my sixth month of pregnancy. I knew the extra weight was causing pressure on my spine. I assumed Dr. Palmer was going to prescribe medication that would relieve my pain and not affect my baby.

Yet again, I was wrong. I got dressed and walked down the hallway into her office. She said, "Victoria, please have a seat." As I sat down, she placed three pamphlets in front of me. She looked at me and said, "Mommy, you are experiencing a high-risk pregnancy, and these pamphlets will explain what to expect during a high-risk pregnancy."

I said, "Oh God! Please, Dr. Palmer, don't tell me I am going to lose my baby!" Tears began to flow from my eyes as I gently rubbed my stomach. In the back of my mind, I could hear Dr. Smith's voice echoing, "You may never experience childbirth." I said with a tremble in my voice, "Dr. Palmer, I love this little boy more than life! I will do anything to bring him into this world. Tell me what I need to do." My hands were trembling. I tried to wipe the tears from my eyes, yet they continued to flow.

Dr. Palmer walked around from her desk and hugged me in an effort to console me. She said, "Victoria, I know this is an unfortunate situation, but you have to remain calm for you and your son."

After a few minutes, I was calm enough to comprehend the orders that she gave me. Dr. Palmer looked at me and said, "If you want a healthy baby, you must do exactly what my orders instruct you to do." She said that I was experiencing premature labor and my back pain was caused by contractions. She informed me that I was dilated four centimeters and my cervix was soft. She said, "Victoria, you must remain on complete bed rest. If not, you will be placed in the hospital until you deliver your son. You cannot walk, run, exercise, or engage in any sexual activity." She wrote me a prescription for terbutaline once a day. Dr. Palmer informed me that the medication was used in order to stop or delay preterm labor. It also helps prevent and slow contractions of the uterus. Dr. Palmer registered my phone number with the high-risk clinic.

I was issued a device that had a small monitor attached, it was similar to a large belt. I wore the device twenty-four hours a day. A nurse from the high-risk clinic called me every afternoon in order to record the number of contractions I experienced within twenty-four hours. I can recall so clearly how I would remove the monitor from my stomach and place it on the telephone receiver. I would switch the button from "On" to "Read." There was a click followed by two to three minutes of a humming sound. After the noise ceased, the nurse would inform me of how many contractions I had the day before. The most I've recorded were fifteen to twenty contractions in twenty-four hours.

I did exactly what the pamphlets informed me to do, as well as what Dr. Palmer ordered. My prayer warriors and I prayed every morning together. On January 6, 1987, God blessed me with one of his angels. My son was born handsome and healthy. The love of my life weighed in at seven pounds five ounces. He is now a grown man with an amazing wife who has a heart of gold and a smile that lights the entire room. I love her as much as I love my daughter.

Nine years later, I was elated to find out that I was pregnant with my daughter. She was also high risk. Once again, I was placed on bed rest. I was older and more experienced concerning high-risk pregnancies. I was worried but not devastated as I was before. I went in for my six-month checkup with Dr. Peterson. He informed me that I had to report to Texas Women Hospital because I was in labor and my daughter was in distress. I arrived at the hospital and was immediately given an epidural because of the severity of my contractions. Dr. Ang informed me that he was going to perform an emergency Cesarean section. If not, my daughter would not survive. I went into surgery within two hours of my arrival. My best friend, Sarah, was there to pray with me as she had been through most of my surgeries.

I went into surgery shortly after she arrived. Dr. Ang walked into the room and said, "Mom, it's February 7, 1996, and we're going to deliver a baby girl today." I felt him pulling my daughter from my stomach; it wasn't painful but was very uncomfortable. About ten to fifteen minutes later, I heard the sweetest sound in the world: my daughter's cry.

Shortly afterward, I heard Dr. Ang yell, "I need pediatric ICU right now!" I was covered from my neck down with sheets and could not see him until I looked over my right shoulder. Dr. Ang had my daughter wrapped in a blanket, and he ran out of the room holding her close to his chest. I tried to ask my husband what was happening. He leaned over, kissed me, and assured me that everything would be okay. I tried to get off the table, but I was temporarily paralyzed because of the epidural. The last thing I remember, before they administered more anesthesia, was telling my husband to go find my baby girl. When I awoke, it felt as though I was asleep for a few minutes. Greg was sitting in a chair next to the bed, holding my hand. He told me I was asleep for several hours. Shortly after I awoke, the nurse came into my room. She helped me into a wheelchair and transported me to pediatric ICU. My daughter was three months premature. She weighed less than 4 pounds. Her ears were not developed. She did not have toenails or fingernails. There was an indentation in her chest. Her breathing was extremely shallow.

I could not touch or hold my daughter. Three days later, I was released from the hospital, but I had to leave my precious angel in NICU because she was extremely ill and underweight. Less than a week in NICU, I received a phone call. The nurse informed me she would have to administer a feeding tube into my daughter because she refused to drink Enfamil with iron. I asked the nurse if I could try to feed my daughter before they placed another tube inside of her, and she agreed.

My husband and I arrived at the hospital within the hour. Before I walked into the NICU nursery, I went into the bathroom and slowly got on my knees because I was cut from hip to hip because of the Cesarean section. I began praying, "God, you said in Deuteronomy 32:39, 'See now that I myself am he! There is no God besides me. I put to death and I bring to life, I have wounded and I will heal, and no one can deliver out of my hand.'

"God, I know you would not trust me with your angel only to take her away from me. Father, you know how much I can bear. You know my strength.

"Father, you have given me so much love to give. Please allow me to share the love you have given me with my son and daughter. God, they are all I have in this world. I am blessed with family, friends, and a wonderful husband. My children grew inside of me. They will forever be mine. Please, God, I ask in your name let your will be done."

I scrubbed my hands and went into the nursery. As I stood at my daughter's side, the nurse asked me if I would try to pump for my daughter because she did not have any more milk and I could not produce milk less than three hours ago. I asked the nurse for my breast pump. I went into the room, turned the pump on, placed it on my breast, and milk began flowing as though I had never stopped pumping. Tears began to roll down my face. I began thanking God. You see, I knew at the moment my precious Princess was going to be okay.

Back to My Ovarian Surgery

M y ovarian surgery was very painful. Dr. Smith had to cut me from hip to hip because of the large number of cysts he removed. Recovery was very painful and challenging. It hurt to sneeze, cough, laugh, or relieve myself. He assured me that recovery would take six to eight weeks. Unfortunately, my body took over twelve weeks to heal. Again, when family and friends came over, they continued to tell me that I didn't look sick. I did not look as though I was cut from hip to hip. I said I wish it were all a joke, but unfortunately it's 100 percent reality.

As I began leading a normal life as a young adult—working, hanging out with my friends, and going to the movies, parties, and football games—I began to relax. A year passed, and I decided not to return to school, but I needed more for my life.

Oh My God, I Had Cancer

I decided to join the Houston Police Department. Their paper-work requested that I obtain a copy of my medical records. My mom drove me to Diagnostic Hospital in order for me to do so. As she was driving, I was reading my medical summary. I said, "Oh my God, this sentence states that I had a cancerous tumor removed from my left breast at sixteen years of age." I said, "Mom, I had breast cancer!"

She said yes.

Emotions began to consume me. I was angry because no one told me. I was afraid that it might return. I was grateful that I was in remission. I was confused because I went through treatment, but I never realized what was happening to me. I said, "Mom this is very difficult to comprehend."

She said, "Victoria, when you read you had cancer, what was your immediate thought?"

I said, "Why didn't anyone tell me I had cancer? I could have died."

She said, "Exactly. Your dad and I decided not to tell you because we did not want your faith to turn into fear. When you were sick and weak, I saw the strength in you when we assured you that you were okay. Do you recall after radiation treatments you would eat chicken broth?"

I said yes.

My mom said the doctor told her that I would not be able to eat anything, yet I looked forward to chicken broth after my procedures. She said she was not going to allow anyone to set limitations for me and I should allow God to shine through me—always allow others to see my glory, not my story.

As years passed and it appeared as though everyone I knew from high school was preparing for their college graduation or engagements, I began to feel that I was not in control of my life. My appearance was no longer satisfying to me. My hair was too short. My nose was too big. My eyes were too wide. Every time I looked in the mirror, it appeared as though I weighed over three hundred pounds. I began eating salads with no dressing. I ran five miles a day.

Recovering from anorexia

When I began to take control of my life, I weighed 145lbs. I lost thirty-five pounds in a matter of months. I thought to myself that if I worked out and ate less, maybe I would become slim and healthy. I thought of Psalm 139:14: "I praise you because I am fearfully and wonderfully made; your works are wonderful." I felt guilty because deep within my heart I wasn't wonderfully made. I know that we all are created in the image of God, and God doesn't make imperfections. We are all masterpieces in our Father's eyes.

I was confused because I wanted to take control of my health. I was afraid to commit to anything in fear of becoming ill and having to walk away from my dream or passion. I believe in God, His goodness, and His mercy; however, this made sense to me because it appeared as though eating and working out were the only way I had control of my life.

I recalled the day when I took a bowl of soup out of the refrigerator, and as I reached for a pot to warm it, my mom grabbed the bowl and asked me if I was aware that I had been eating on the same bowl of soup for two days. Most people prepared a can of soup and complete it in one meal. I would eat three spoons of soup a day and add water to the bowl afterward. She insisted that I talk to a counselor because it appeared as though I was obsessed with being smaller, yet no matter how much weight I lost, it was never enough.

I could not believe my mom was considering counseling because she believed Psalms 16:7–8: "I will praise the LORD who counsels me—even at night my conscience instructs me. I keep the LORD in mind always. Because He is at my right hand, I will not be shaken." My dad explained to Mom that the glory of God is true and righteous but we have godly brothers and sisters who can also help us in time of hardships.

My mom reached out to a Christian counselor. We talked about my past and why I felt so vulnerable and out of control. He told me that I appeared to be suffering from depression, which can lead to anorexia. I had never heard of anorexia before. He informed me that the exact causes of anorexia nervosa were unknown. However, the condition is sometimes hereditary. We were also informed that a person's psychological, environmental, and social factors may contribute to the development of anorexia. People with anorexia come to believe that their lives would be better if only they were thinner. These people tend to be perfectionists and overachievers. In fact, the typical anorexic person is a good student involved in school and community activities. Many experts think that anorexia is part of an unconscious attempt to come to terms with unresolved conflicts or painful childhood experiences. I assured him that the only pain I felt as a child was continuous illness and hospitalizations. I had no control. I tried to remain prayerful and faithful to God, yet it seemed as though I have failed once again.

During prayer and counseling, I began to eat more, which was very difficult for me. The journey was tough, yet I did not travel it alone. My family was there to encourage and pray with me. I was not aware of the damage that I caused to my body. It wasn't until I became a Houston police officer that I began to notice the toll that my eating disorder took on my previously weak and unhealthy body.

Oh, God, Please Heal My Heart

I graduated from the Houston Police Department Academy Class 138. I was the only African American female in that class. I knew I had to do well because so many eyes were on me. I will admit the academy was very difficult for me. Oftentimes I would awake with a stomachache, but I had to pray and ask God for strength to make it through the day. No one really knew how weak and lethargic I felt. My body wasn't nearly as healthy as my classmates'. After physical training, during lecture, I would feel myself becoming nauseous; but I would zone out, go into prayer, and miss most of the lecture. It was God and his grace that bought me through.

After graduation I was assigned to Southwest Patrol Command where I met my second family: Anthony, John, Christopher, Joann, Elaine, and Diane. I will never forget our days on patrol together. I recall one morning after roll call, I noticed that my friend wasn't herself. She's not a person of few words. I was assigned to the radio room. This is part of the desk officers' assignment. I issued her a radio, bean bag shotgun, laptop computer, and keys to her patrol car. She said thank you. I said, *Oh no, something is wrong.*

We talked every morning for at least thirty minutes after roll call. I followed her outside and asked her if she needed to talk. We sat in her car, and she explained to me that she was afraid because the doctor found a small lump in her breast. She began to cry. We hugged, and I asked her if I could show her something. She wiped the tears from her eyes and said yes. We walked back into the station and went into the ladies' bathroom. Without revealing my entire breast, I showed her the scars on both of my breasts. I told her that

I am a breast cancer survivor. I asked her the common questions on breast cancer signs and symptoms, which included skin changes, swelling, redness, or other visible differences in one or both breasts. Was there an increase in size or change in the shape of the breast(s)? Were there changes in the appearance of one or both nipples? Did she notice nipple discharge? I also asked her if she was experiencing any pain in any part of the breast. She answered no to the general questions. I'm not a doctor or nurse, and I do not profess myself to be. I was trying to recall the questions that Dr. Smith asked me. She said, "I never knew you were a survivor. You look so healthy, happy, and upbeat. Looking at you, I would have never thought you experienced such a traumatic time in your life." She asked me why I never mentioned it before.

I said there was no reason to say anything until now. "It's not about me. It's about you and your healing. I want you to believe in your healing." I pulled out a prayer card from my uniform pocket. It read:

> Jesus,
> With just one touch from your Almighty creative
>   hand,
> You have healed the sick and raised the dead.
> How amazing is Your Lordship over all the earth,
> How powerful is Your redeeming love.
> How great was Your sacrifice to go before us and
>   bring forgiveness and hope.
> By Your stripes I ask for healing.
> Standing within Your reign and rule I ask for
>   restoration.

We also directed our attention to Exodus 23:25: "Worship the LORD your God, and His blessing will be on your food and water. I will take away sickness from among you."

A few days passed, and she called and told me that her biopsy revealed that her cyst was not cancerous. That was one of most unforgettable moments at Southwest Patrol. After my friend's procedure, she was assigned to work the front desk with me until her stitches healed.

It was a peaceful Saturday morning. We were booking in class C misdemeanor prisoners. Class C misdemeanors resulted in a fine of $200 or less. The station phone rang, and I answered in my usual greeting, "Southwest Patrol, Officer Johnson, how I can help you?" The voice on the other end sounded horrific. All I understood was "Oh God! Oh God! Help me, God! Oh Jesus!" followed by tear-jerking screams of agony and sheer heartbroken pain.

I said, "Ma'am, please calm down." I was terrified by her plea for help, but I learned that when everything around you falls apart, breathe, pray, and maintain control of the situation. I couldn't tell her to hang up and call 911 because I was afraid if we disconnected her life would be over. I said, "Ma'am, you have to calm down. Where are you calling from? What is the address? Are you in danger? Is there anyone else there with you? Do you need an ambulance?"

Again she yelled, "Oh God, please not my babies! Please, God, not my babies! Baby, help me! Please help me! I don't know what to do!"

I said, "Mamma, is that you?"

She said, "Yes! Yes, it's me! Help me, baby! Please help Mamma!" It was my mother on the other end of the phone.

I threw the phone down, grabbed my keys, and literally jumped over the front desk. I ran to the parking lot in hopes of getting into my car. As I was running through the parking lot, another officer twice my size stopped me and said, "I'm driving. Just tell me what you need and where to go."

I was crying! I said, "Dispatch a unit to my parents' house. I need them code 1 lights and siren. This is an emergency."

He said, "Consider it done, baby girl."

Our estimated time of arrival to my parents' house was thirty to forty minutes. We arrived in less than twelve minutes. I jumped out of the car. I almost fell because the car was still in motion. As I was running to my parents' front door, I pulled my gun from my holsters.

As I approached the door, I stopped. I yelled out for my mom. She said, "I'm here. It's your sister! It's your sister! They said she's going to die!"

I ran into the kitchen and saw my mom lying in a fetal position with her panties and bra on. I had never seen my mom in such despair and vulnerability. I knew that I had to be her rock just as she was mine for so many years. I said, "Mamma, look at me. Stop! Look into my eyes! You are not alone! God brought me safely to you! Whatever it is, our God, my God, your God will get us through this no matter what." I did not yell or cry. I reminded her that we were in this together, but she had to talk to me and tell me what was going on.

She said, "I received a call from Dothan, Alabama. While on their way to Walt Disney World, they were involved in an accident. Your sister, brother in-law, and two nephews are dead or dying."

I wanted to scream. It felt as though my mom stabbed me in my heart with a butter knife and pulled it from my chest. Yet I was able to keep my composure because she was depending on my strength and faith as I depended on hers for so many years. I breathed and called on Jesus. I said, "Mom, who called you with this information?"

She said, "The nurse from the hospital."

I said, "What hospital?"

She said, "I'm not sure. When she told me, I threw the phone down and called you."

I said, "Jesus, please help me!"

Less than five seconds later, the nurse from the hospital called back. The officer who drove me to my parents' house told me that he would get all the necessary information. He said, "You need to take care of your mom."

I took my mom into the bathroom and dressed her, and we prayed the Twenty-Third Psalm, "The Lord is my shepherd. I shall not want. He makes me lie down in green pastures. He leads me beside still waters. He restores my soul. He leads me in paths of righteousness for His name's sake. Even though I walk through the valley of the shadow of death, I will fear no evil, for You are with me. Your rod and Your staff, they comfort me. You prepare a table before me in the presence of my enemies. You anoint my head with oil. My cup overflows. Surely goodness and mercy shall follow me all the days of my life, and I shall dwell in the house of the Lord forever."

While we were praying, I could honestly say that I felt calmness throughout the entire room. My mom's breathing calmed down. Her body was no longer shivering. She stopped crying. I said, "Mom, are you okay?" Yet the entire time I wanted to explode, but I couldn't because I knew she needed me more than ever. I thanked God for giving me the strength to endure because this situation was much bigger than I could handle.

We walked back into the kitchen where the officer was taking notes from the nurse in Alabama. He asked her if anyone was deceased, and she said, "No, not at this time. However, the entire family is in the critical care unit, and we are not sure if they will make it until the next morning."

I took a deep breath. I called the airlines and explained my situation. They explained to me that they reserved seats for hardship cases. I made reservations, and my mom and I were on a flight within four hours of that horrific phone call. We arrived at the hospital; and my sister, brother in-law, and nephews were in intensive care. The highway patrolman informed us that while traveling down the interstate, the rubber flew from the front right tire of their Ford Explorer. My brother in-law lost control of the vehicle, which went across three lanes of traffic; hit a tree; and rolled into a ditch. My middle nephew was ejected from the vehicle. He landed on his back, damaged his spine, and punctured his lungs. Glass was imbedded into his legs, head, and neck. My sister's leg, pelvis, and arm were crushed. The prong from the headrest stabbed my brother-in-law in the back of the head. He was coughing and spitting blood. My oldest nephew's knee was crushed, and his lung was punctured. The doctors told us that the most critical time for each of them was the next seventy-two hours.

My mom and I stayed at the hospital for three days. We showered, ate, and prayed at the hospital by my sister's and her family's side. The fourth day in ICU, my nephews were released into a private room. My sister and brother in-law remained in the ICU. After four weeks in the hospital, my nephews were released to travel back to Houston. Honestly, I had no idea how I was going to travel with two teenagers in wheelchairs, one with a body cast and the other with a full leg cast. My mom and I prayed together before our flight home. She assured me that she would be okay. I returned to Houston, and it was extremely overwhelming once the flight landed. I could not believe my eyes. My extended family from the Houston Police Department were there waiting for me with wheelchairs, gift bags, and gift cards. It was extremely overwhelming.

Two months later, my sister and brother in-law returned home. The road to recovery was challenging, tiring, and extremely emotional; yet again, through God and his grace, they made a full recovery. I returned back to work several weeks later. I was assigned to patrol.

While on patrol, I had the opportunity to meet wonderful people who were in very bad situations. Most of my area was single-parent homes, foster homes, and/or government housing. Society has put a label on high-crime areas, yet most of the crime was being committed by individuals outside of their community. Most people in my district and beat were loyal and respectful. I can recall the worst dispatched call of my career, which caused me to work the front desk. It was the murder of a teenager. The young man was running away from a group of guys who jumped on him, and they shot him several times in the back. The young man died in my arms with his eyes open. Yet there was nothing I could do for him. I will forever remember the look on his face when he took his last breath. That incident will never leave my heart or my thoughts. The young man who killed him was sentenced and convicted of murder. As I held the victim in my arms, I recalled the walk that my mom and I took through Ben Taub emergency room. I asked God to give his family mercy and strength to endure.

Front desk, Southwest Patrol

Shortly after the incident, the captain of Southwest Patrol assigned me to the desk for two weeks. I was sitting at the front desk, completing an accident report, when my sergeant walked in the back door of the station. He asked me if I liked his haircut. I looked up at him, and we both started laughing. It appeared as though his barber edged his hair an inch farther than his hairline. When I reached out to touch his hair, I felt a pain in my chest that almost knocked me to the floor. It felt as though a twenty-pound weight were sitting on my chest. We both thought it was indigestion. He went into the break room to buy me a Coke. As he was walking out, a female officer was walking in. The pain was getting more intense, and it was now hard for me to breathe. I asked the officer to take me to St. Luke's Hospital because it was less than ten minutes away. She drove with her emergency equipment on, lights and siren. I'm sure we arrived in less than five minutes.

Once we arrived, she jumped out of the car, ran into the ER, and yelled, "I NEED HELP! A police officer is having a heart attack."

Four people in scrubs ran out to the patrol car. I was sitting in the passenger seat with my feet on the ground. I was trying to gather enough strength to stand. A female nurse looked at me and said, "Where is the officer who's having chest pains?"

I said in a low whisper while holding my chest, "It's me."

She looked at me and said, "You don't look like you are having chest pains."

I told her, "I'm not sure how chest-pain patients look, but my chest is hurting, and it is difficult to walk and breathe."

The male nurse ran out with a wheelchair and rolled me to an examining room. The nurse immediately placed an oxygen mask over my mouth and nose. She placed an IV on the back of my hand and drew several vials of blood. My blood pressure was elevated. She placed patches on my chest in order to obtain a reading of my heart activity. After the EKG, she asked if my family was in the waiting room. She began a series of questions, "Do you smoke, drink, or are you under more pressure than normal?" I answered no to all the questions. As she recorded the results from the EKG machine, she asked if I had a history of heart disease in my family. Again, I answered no.

The nurse informed me that the doctor would be in shortly. I had no idea what was going on until the doctor came in and gave me a small pill. He instructed me to place it under my tongue. He said it was a nitroglycerin pill that would help ease the pain. After the pill dissolved, my chest pain stopped almost immediately, but it caused me to have a severe migraine—nothing like I have ever felt before. It sounded as though he was yelling when he was talking. The beeping on the medical devices sounded like sirens on emergency vehicles. I was able to block the noise out. I forced myself to sit up on the side of the bed. I told the doctor that I felt better. I would schedule a follow-up with my primary care physician once I returned to the police station.

He looked at me and said, "I'm sorry, Mrs. Johnson, but you are going to be admitted into our cardiac observation unit."

I said, "CARDIAC OBSERVATION UNIT! Sir, that's for people with suspected heart problems. Just prescribe me some of those nitroglycerin pills. I will take one when needed, and I will be fine."

He informed me the problem was, the pill made me feel better, which gave him the indication that my heart was in distress. He said, "Your blood test, EKG, and chief complaint were sure signs of a mild heart attack."

"Oh God!" I became so anxious that it caused my blood pressure to elevate. The monitor went off; the nurse walked in, and asked if I was okay. The doctor told me that he was going to contact the cardiac unit in order for them to prepare me a bed. I told the nurse that I was afraid because my family wasn't with me. I asked her to call the chaplain. She agreed to do so. The nurse also informed me that St. Luke specialized in cardiovascular research, and if anything was to happen, they would be there in less than a minute. When she said that, I thought about Joshua 1:5: "No man shall be able to stand before you all the days of your life. Just as I was with Moses, so I will be with you. I will not leave you or forsake you." I'm not alone because God has never left my side.

As I was praying, the chaplain walked in. He introduced himself and asked if he could pray with me. I said, "You can pray with me and for me." He smiled and said, "You are a child of God. No matter what the outcome of your visit is, you are going to be blessed. I felt the Holy Spirit as I walked into this room."

He began to pray James 5:15, "And the prayer of faith shall save the sick, and the Lord shall raise him up, and if he has committed sins, they shall be forgiven him."

After prayer, we began to talk about God and His grace. We talked about how He walked with Moses, Paul, David, and Peter. We even talked about the Bible story of the Prodigal Son. I told him that a friend of mine, during Bible study, made a valid point. He said the

Bible story should have been titled "The Forgiving Father" because the father forgave the son for all his wrongdoings and welcomed him home with open arms. The chaplain thought that was very profound, and so did I. The chaplain's presence and prayers relaxed me until my family arrived. Once they arrived, the officer and chaplain left. My brother looked at me and said, "You don't look like you had a mild heart attack. Matter of fact, you don't look sick."

My mom reached over and put her hand on his knee and said, "When people look at you, they should see your glory and not your story. Always let God's light shine through you, not the trials that you encounter throughout your life."

After spending a few days in the hospital, I returned home on bed rest for a week. Everything at work was going great. A year passed, and I was back on track with my life.

Horseback Riding to Back Surgery

My husband and I decided to take a trip to Padre Island near Corpus Christi, Texas. We went horseback riding on the beach. After the ride, I tried to get off the horse, but I could not walk. The pain was so severe my husband had to carry me to the car. I took six Aleve tablets, but the pain did not subside. When we returned to Houston, he drove me to St. Luke's emergency room. They were able to stop the pain. I had several X-rays and blood tests. The results showed a large synovial cyst on my spine. I had severe degenerative disease in my cervical and lumbar spine. I also had a herniated disc in my L4 and L5. I was unable to walk because the nerve damage caused severe weakness in my left leg. I was confined to a wheelchair, and the doctor told me that surgery was needed. He told me that it was a blessing that we rode horses because it agitated the cyst, which attached itself to my nerves for over a year. They provided me with a wheelchair and several strong pain medications until my surgery was scheduled. My surgery was nine hours, and a total of seventy-five staples were placed in my back. Less than a week prior to this incident, I was totally independent.

Now I'm totally dependent on my family. I was off from work for eight months. I was afraid to return because I knew if I received a severe impact to my back, I may never walk again. Physical therapy was extremely painful, yet I was determined with God as my guide to overcome another obstacle. When I felt despondent, I would tell myself, *Your setback is preparing you for an even better comeback.* I thought about Psalm 121:1: "I look to the hills which cometh my help, my help comes from the Lord."

After the extensive therapy and special diets, I returned to work. I was assigned to Sex Offenders Registration, where my niece also worked as a Houston police officer. During my back-surgery recovery, she became my personal psychiatrist. She listened to me when I was down. She came over, sat in bed, and ate lunch with me every Friday. She would look over at me, smile, and say, "Girl, you are my ride or die even if you can't walk." We both would laugh. She would fill me in on everything that was going on in the office. Unfortunately, my time in Sex Offender's Registration was one year and three months. I was transferred to Juvenile Intake Missing Person nightshift. My shift was nights from 10:00 p.m. to 6:00 a.m.

My daughter was the victim of bullying. She was in the seventh grade. The day that I received evidence that she was being laughed at and taunted by several girls in her gym class, I withdrew her the same day. I enrolled her into K-12. It's an accredited school that met the needs of families wishing to homeschool their child or children. I was exhausted, but my daughter received a quality education, and our mother-daughter bond grew stronger.

I met my current pastor and several other amazing officers while working in Juvenile Intake. It was less than ten of us assigned to the unit. On Thursday before work, we would meet upstairs and discuss our midweek Bible study lessons. There were two ministers who were a part of our discussions, and I must admit both were very knowledgeable. I would ask questions and give examples concerning a particular scripture. Oftentimes I would be off topic; however, they didn't have the heart to say, "Go home and study more." They were extremely patient with me. They answered questions and gave examples until that lightbulb would glow through my eyes, you know, the "oh, okay, I get it now" look that many of us experience after being confused for so long and finally we are on the same page with everyone else. We talked about Bible stories, Bible verses, and power of prayer. We shared our tests as well as our testimonies.

One day I woke up and was preparing for work and Bible study. I was in severe pain. I could barely walk. The doctor said it was to be expected because of the hardware that was installed into my spine.

I felt it was time to do what I wanted to do because life was not guaranteed. After twenty-five years of service with the Houston Police Department, it was time for me to retire and teach elementary school. I began working on my teaching certification. A month before I completed Texas Teachers, I decided to retire from the police department. I was strong mentally and physically. I had never felt better. I was hired at Frost Elementary, which, in my opinion, is one of the best schools in the Lamar Consolidated School District; and the leadership there was impeccable.

Only four months into my new career, which I extremely enjoyed, I was walking down the hall and my left leg became weak. I fell against the wall. I tried to play it off, but my friend Patricia noticed, and she made me promise that I would see a doctor. I made an appointment with my primary care doctor. She ordered X-rays and later an MRI. She told me that I had to see a neurologist. I saw the neurologist, and he informed me that another back surgery and neck surgery were needed. I did not ask any questions. I received a second and third opinion, and all agreed that I was suffering from another synovial cyst on my spine. I had spondylolisthesis, which is a condition that causes a bone in your spine to protrude out farther than the other bones, causing pressure on your spinal cord or nerves; and the degenerative disc disease was worse. I contacted the assistant principal via email and informed her that I would not be returning to work. Writing my letter of resignation was very painful because I loved my job and the people I worked with, but most of all, the children were amazing. I cried as I put my circumstances into writing. This is what I said:

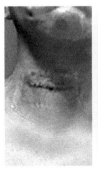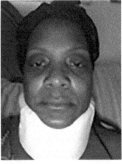

I hope you enjoyed the holiday season. I am reaching out to you with the latest information concerning the status of my health; I am going to have another back surgery. Initially, I was told that a chance of returning back to work was possible. I spoke to my doctor today in hopes of receiving a Return to Work statement. Unfortunately, I was informed by my doctor that I could not return unless certain restrictions were abided by. He informed that my MRI revealed narrowing of my spinal canal, and further progression of the severe degenerative disc disease. It is imperative that I attend physical therapy 3 times a week, and do everything I can to limit the pressure on my spine. He also stated that he will not provide me with a work release unless I adhere to several limitations; I would be required to use a specialized orthopedic chair, and to limit my walking, sitting, and standing. Still, resource's job description requires me to perform effectively and efficiently; I know that my limited mobility will not be sufficient. I do not feel that I can service the students due to my health. They deserve the best, and I can no longer provide them with my best.

I know that I have not allowed you enough time to fill my position, and I sincerely apologize for that. You guys have been amazing to me; I cannot stress my appreciation enough. Although my abilities are now restricted, I want to do what's best considering my situation. I'm curious to know what you feel would be most sufficient in this instance. I truly apologize for any inconvenience but I thank you wholeheartedly for believing in me, and for being so patient with me through all of this. These diagnoses have not been easy on my heart, nor on my spirit. Your empathy and encouragement has done more than you could ever imagine. I am grateful and very appreciative.

Although it was very difficult for me to resign, I must say that I am at peace with my life. Most people pray for money, fame, and/or notoriety. My prayer for my family is that God gives them an abundant amount of peace because with peace, your spiritual, emotional, financial, and physical needs are met to your expectations. I have more peace in my life than I have ever experienced.

I thank God for blessing me with my husband, lover, and friend. His name is Gregory Wayne Johnson. We have been together for over twenty-five years. We have experienced good and bad times, yet Greg has never left my side. When I was unable to help myself, he would feed and bathe me. When I could not walk, he carried me. Whenever the pain became too difficult for me to bear, he continued to remind me that his shoulders were made for me to lean on. He was there by my side during every surgery; I love and appreciate him for being there for me no matter what situation we are faced with. He's not perfect, and neither am I; but I pray that our daughter will marry a man like her father, a man who will love and respect her unconditionally.

Our Revive Bible Church family has been there to assist my family through the good, bad, and indifferent times. Pastor Latin has blessed both my grandsons. He continues to pray for our health as well as our marriages. My prayer is when others read my story, they will see that they are not alone. So many times I felt as though I was being punished. I felt I wasn't living up to God's expectations. I wanted to give up and just stand; but please understand that life can be cruel and painful, and most of the times you don't know what you are going to do. Please never stop praying and believing in God and his word.

I recall an older lady telling me that the Bible was our **B**asic **I**nstructions **B**efore **L**eaving **E**arth. I'm a strong believer in her words. You see, God has a way of placing us in situations and circumstances in order to help and heal us. I thank him for my testimonies and his undying love. Sometimes life becomes uncomfortable in order for us to see our blessings.

My entire life has always been encapsulated with one test after another. Throughout my tests, I witnessed amazing testimonies.

God turned my test into a testimony.

My son Ronnie, whom I thought I was going to experience a miscarriage at six months of my pregnancy, is an amazing father and husband. They are active members of Revive Bible Church. Ronnie is very smart and determined; and recently he received an award and a promotion on his job for leadership, excellence, and dependability. Ronnie and Tiffany are Mason's soccer and baseball coaches. They cheer him on weekly in karate. Whatever my grandson participates in, they attend the event as a family. I frequently explain to them how proud I am. He often reminds me of Proverbs 22:6: "Train up a child in the way he should go; even when he is old he will not depart from it."

Approximately ten years ago, my son wrote me a song titled "Thank You Mama." I continue to hold the lyrics dear to my heart. My son has never once made me regret January 6, 1987. If I had to travel that same road again, I would not hesitate. The love I have for him is countless.

Thank you, God, for giving me the strength to pass my test.

God turned another test into a testimony.

My daughter, Princess, was the one I thought I was going to lose because she was rushed to the ICU and fought for her life at a very young age. At three months, she was rushed to the hospital and was diagnosed with ventricular septum defect, which is a common heart defect most often present at birth. It involves a hole in the wall between the heart's lower chambers. She was treated by two different specialists, each informing me that my daughter's heart was normal. Princess and I have developed a mother-daughter bond that I have always dreamed of. My mom has always been my rock, and I will be nothing less for my daughter. Throughout grade school and high school, Princess has won several academic and theater awards. She is the epitome of an amazing daughter. Princess is now an honor's student at Baylor University. She will be graduating May 2018. My daughter has never once made me regret the pain and heartache I felt on February 7, 1996.

Thank you, God, for allowing me to turn another test into a testimony.

God made my health a living testimony.

Breast cancer, mild heart attack, anorexia, abdominal surgery, eye surgery, two back surgeries, neck surgery, fear of never experiencing childbirth, possibility of losing both my children because of my weak and unhealthy body, and resignation from a job that I knew God had in store for me—the list can go on, but I think you understand what I'm saying. My sickness was my test, yet today God has healed me. I'm not where I need to be, but I'm better than what I used to be.

My niece Angel and I walk six miles three times a week. I attend water aerobics twice a week. My best friend, Sarah, and I eat lunch together once a month. My mom, sister, and I attend a girls' day out the first Tuesday of every month. The first of every month, my husband schedules and pays for my full body massage, manicure, and pedicure. I have family and a few friends who I love and receive love from in return. When I retired, Greg surprised me with the car of my dreams. I live in a beautiful home in a gated community. Since retirement, I have traveled to Puerto Rico, Belize, Cozumel, and Montego Bay, Jamaica. I have peace that can't be measured. I feel love that cannot be calculated. I have faith that is unimaginable.

Thank you, God, for all that you have done, will do, and are continuing to do, Most of all, thank you for my tests and my testimonies.

God made my parents strong in order to make me their testimony.

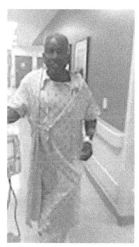

As I stated earlier, my dad was diagnosed with kidney cancer. He is a strong and vibrant seventy-seven-year-old man. I scheduled appointments to three doctors, and each informed me that my dad's tumor was in a very complicated position and surgery was not an option. My dad was nervous and concerned about his health. As we were walking from the doctor's office toward the parking lot, he looked at me with tears in his eyes and said, "Baby what am I going to do?"

I hugged him and told him, "Just pray and let me handle this."

I contacted the Cancer Center Treatment of America. The nurse I spoke with was an angel sent from heaven. She explained to me what signs and symptoms my dad may encounter. Greg and I stayed awake all night searching the internet for the best urologist that Houston has to offer. I cried, I prayed, and I asked God to please lead me to the right physician. I needed a doctor who would see my dad through my eyes. I wanted them to see a man whose heart is pure, a man who worked hard for his family. I did not want a doctor to see a seventy-seven-year-old man with cancer and no hope of recovery. Finally, I came across Dr. Andrew Selzman of the Memorial Hermann Medical Urology Group. I looked at Greg and said, "This is the doctor. I feel it."

I called the following morning. The nurse told me that they had a cancelation and my dad's appointment was scheduled for the next day. Dr. Selzman stated that my dad was one of the healthiest seventy-seven-year-old men he has had the pleasure of meeting. He informed me that the surgery would be complicated, but he felt it would be successful. My dad's surgery was a success. He has been cancer free for two years now. He walks five miles a day and trains weight three times a week.

My mom spends most of her time with me. Since she fell, her memory and balance are not as strong as the doctors would like for them to be. We sit together daily and watch CNN. I'm her legs and her mind. If she needs something, I do not hesitate to make sure she receives it. My sister and I both care for her. My brother is unable to assist in the care for our parents. He made several bad choices as a young adult, and his health has continued to fail him. I will admit that I am proud of the accomplishments that he has made in his later years. He is a child of God and will soon become a certified drug counselor. He has full custody of his twins. "But in their distress they turned to the LORD God of Israel, and they sought Him, and He let them find Him" (2 Chron. 15:4). To God is the glory.

Everywhere I go, my mom wants to ride with me and sit in the car until I return. No matter how long it takes, she will sit and play solitaire on her phone. I have never understood why she does that. Nevertheless, I would do anything in this world for both of them because they have given me their world and my life.

Thank you, God, for giving me the strength to care for my parents.

To God is the glory because when others see me, they see his glory and not my story.

About the Author

*C*arla Johnson is fifty-two years old. She's married to Gregory Johnson. Throughout their twenty-seven years together, they were blessed with a son, daughter, daughter-in-law, and grandson. Carla is a retired Houston police officer with twenty-five years of service. She resigned from education because of a degenerative disc disease. She committed her life to Christ at an early age. She has survived many trials and tribulations. Yet no matter what life has in store for her, she has always turned her tests into testimonies.

CPSIA information can be obtained
at www.ICGtesting.com
Printed in the USA
LVHW092022310520
656911LV00007BA/660